In the Middle of the Night...
A collection of poems
By: Iona Henry

Edited by: Mario A. Thomas
Cover photo by: Juilan Hofer
Cover graphics by: Isaac Márquez

Copyright © 2020 by Iona Henry

All rights reserved. No part of this publication may be reproduced, distributed or transmitted in any form or by any means, without prior written permission.

In the Middle of the Night / Iona Henry -- 1st ed.
3rd printing June 2021
ISBN:978-0-578-81688-3

~ Acknowledgements ~

This book, my life, and journey are dedicated to God and my mother, Mary Carty Henry (1956-2013). She was taken from me at a time when I needed her the most. But while here, she instilled every piece of her being into my soul. All that I am, is a reminder of her sacrificial love. This book is also dedicated to my late father, Leroy A. Henry (1951-2020) whose warmth kept me sane through this life. To my family and friends whom I hold near and dear to my heart, thank you for your love, humility and continued support. Special thanks to my eldest sister, who was my second mother in my darkest hour.

Note to readers: The first section of this book, entitled, "For My Parents," is dedicated solely to my parents. In this section, I express how I've managed to come to terms with losing both parents within the span of seven years. I also reflect on the regret and hurt that comes after losing a loved one. The second section, "For My People," expresses in short, many of the injustices people of color are subjected to and ways in which we cope. "For My Love," the final section, delves into the mind of a multifaceted woman. This section takes a look into the sensual and vulnerable aspects of the soul.

Table of Contents

Part I:
For My Parents..01
In the Middle of the Night… 03
In Hopes of Rest… 04
Darkness… 05
At Night… 06
Sealed 07
Thank you, Daddy..08
Grandchildren…...09
7…..10
Playing Games…...11
Borrow…..12
Time Again…...13
Cast Away…...14
Escape...15
Was I?…..16
Flowers…...17
Suffering 18
What Happened After 19
Life…...20
Death…...21
A.D. 22

Part II:
For My People 23
Rooted… 25
Carry On…...26
When We Were One… 27
BlackNess…...28
Yes, I'm Mixed...29
New Growth… 30
Protection…...31

Part III:
For My Love **33**
Two… 35
Dream Catcher… 36
Crickets… 37
Rough Hand… 38
Sunday Blues… 39
Intimacy… 40
Once Upon a Time… 41

Part I.

For My Parents

"There is never time in the future to work out our salvation.
The challenge is in the moment;
the challenge is always now."

– James Baldwin

In the middle of the night

In the middle of the night
when my heart stops and my mind wanders,
I think of you…

I think of all the things we could have done,
but chose to wait instead.
"Oh, we can go tomorrow."
"Tomorrow is another day."

But Time, she waits for no one.
And I should have learned my lesson the first time,
when Ma had passed away.

But, I didn't,
so now in the middle of the night,
when I think I hear your voices,
my heart stops and my mind wanders.

The voices, they come in peace.
They are only there to remind me that,
"Time, she waits for no one, so use her wisely."

In Hopes of Rest

In hopes of rest, I close my eyes
red, bulging, aching.

In hopes of rest, I close my eyes,
but there is only darkness there.

My eyes have been hallowed out,
misshapen and taken to the grave.

It is your graves they seek refuge,
red, bulging, aching.

My eyes, they are unrecognizable
twisted in pain.

Who notices, will know.

In hopes of rest, I close my eyes
and I can see you again.

Darkness

The darkness that had once surrounded my heart
has now crept its way back in.
This time it didn't need permission,
it was already acquainted.
It already knew where to go and what rooms
to wrap itself within.

It was a little too familiar with its place in my life.
This time I knew that once it burrowed itself into my bosom,
it would take a lifetime to let go,
especially for you, daddy.

The first time darkness had taken over my heart,
it was slow and savage.
This time it was fast and negligent.
The aches were faster, and so was the shame,
"Was I a good daughter?" "Did I make you proud, Daddy?"
I asked, as I served him small bits of apples
from the hospital cafeteria.

He curled his lips into a crooked smile,
"You were. You always did your best."
A tear slid down my cheek,
for I knew in that moment, he would never lie to me.

At Night

The screeching of the hardwood floor,
   the cynical thoughts of new life.

The empty caskets I hope to find,
   until I am awakened at night.

The steady weeping of the willow,
   the manic cries on my pillow.

The empty feelings I hope to lose,
   until I am awakened at night.

The chills, the screams, the horrid dreams,
   the memories I try to leave behind,
   until I am awakened at night.

At night is when the horror begins.

Sealed

Sealed in this moment in time,
I am meant to be here.

The stairs are connected to elevators.
I push each button,
and yet, I am stuck here.

Frozen in time, sealed in this moment,
I see our faces
glossy and soaking with tears.

The rooms are isolated and drenched in fear.

It is the year of COVID,
yet this is the furthest thing from my mind.

Sealed in this moment in time,
I watch again as you take your last breath,
and your eyes dim their light.

Thank you, Daddy

Thank you for the sanity you have granted me,
it is the sanity I now grant myself.

Thank you for the love you've shared with me,
it is the love I now share with someone else.

Thank you for being my father, confidant, and friend.

Thank you for showing me how to respect myself,
so I can respect everyone else.

Thank you, Daddy
for your unyielding love and sacrifice,
I can now be myself.

Grandchildren

My children will only know you as a folklore, a fable, a myth.
Someone who is talked about often, but is never seen.

My children will ask about you,
they will want to know if you really did exist.

And I will tell them you did, many years ago,
I will tell them everything I know.

You were a God-fearing man, a man with the purest soul.
You sacrificed much for the people you loved,
and even the ones you didn't know.

I wish you could be there, to speak for yourself,
and to watch them grow.

But all I'll have are pictures,
to show them the greatest man I had ever known.

7

Seven was your favorite number.
So, I guess that's why you transitioned on the 7th day,
7 years after your true love went away.

Seven was your number of peace.
The number you used in secret places,
you'd count to seven instead of ten.
You found that number sacred.

I'd remember you telling me,
"The number 7 is divine, it's God's complete number."
And I kept that fact in mind.

I won't use that number for vanity or even in vain,
I'll just remember that it was my daddy's favorite number,
for when I see you again.

Playing Games

My father and I had our own special way of bonding.
We'd play a little game I like to call, pretend.
I'd pretend that my mother's death didn't haunt me,
while he'd pretend that white Jesus would save him
from an impending demise.

He'd pray and pray and pray, thinking that this disease that
respected no man or god,
would somehow go away.
His faith was bigger than his humble spirit,
but in the end, we were both just playing pretend.

I'd pretend that I believed that he was doing, "Just fine."
Because the answers that came after
would have been too hard to bear.

"Daddy are you lying to me?"
Would lay stagnant on my tongue, refusing to leave my lips.
Those types of questions weren't permitted where I grew up,
but I felt as if you knew more.

There were a lot of things left unsaid,
but our bond is stronger than life itself.
And I know I'll dream of you,
and then, you will have no choice but to tell me the truth.

While in another realm, in another life,
we continue to play pretend.

Borrow

We live on borrowed time.

Borrowed minutes, turn to borrowed hours,
as we live our borrowed lives.

Give and give and give and give, I give my borrowed time.
Until one day I have none left.
"Can I get back more of mine?"

No, we can never get back the time we've wasted
on people who don't seem to care.

Borrowed minutes, turn to borrowed hours,
there is never time to spare.

Time Again

Time and time again, we expected Time to be our friend.

We stood still and waited,
as everything around us faded.

We expected Time to sit and wait,
but it just flew, and sealed our faith.

Time is a thief of joy,
a thief of pride.

Sly and coy
Time creeps up, fast.

Turning boys to stone,
and girls to glass.

Time takes away our innocence.

We stop dreaming, we go to work, we retire, and sure enough
we die.

And just like that,
in the blink of an eye,
Time took away you and I.

Cast Away

Cast into the depths of hell,
my mind plays tricks on me.

I see what you see, but do you see me?

Distant in a sea of despair.
The things I had once hoped for,
I no longer seem to care.

Cast into the depths of hell,
my mind plays tricks on me.

The ones who had once nurtured me,
have been taken up in the rapture,
lost, forever, to me alone.

Gone, but not forgotten,
you have found your eternal home.

Yet, I have been cast away,
forever lost to roam.

Escape

When I was a child, my place of escape
was the island across the sea.
Although it was never home, its serenity comforted me.

The turquoise beaches relinquished me of sin,
it was my oasis, my saving grace, my peace within.

Now that I am grown, it's a place of reality and strife,
the streets run red from hate and crime.

But more importantly, now when I'm across the sea,
I'm reminded that you're not here.
Your tombs are filled with fragments of my heart and soul.

Mom and Dad, you were both my true escape,
and now that I'm alone,
I'm not sure where to go.

I guess I can linger here, in purgatory, until it's my time.
But until then, I will continue to seek a new place of escape.

Was I?

Was I your burden that led you to die?

Or was it the stress of everyday life?

You took care of everyone, except for yourself.

Your husband, your kids, grandkids,

and even strangers you had just met.

You were my superwoman, my rock and my strength.

Until one day, out of the blue,

kryptonite finally got a hold of you.

And the life I had once cherished was drained forever,

I was left alone, without a mother.

I wish you could come back and reassure me,

that I was not your kryptonite, disguised in a veil.

Flowers

I wish that I had pulled sweet sage and mint

from out the garden,

and yanked on hibiscuses as their red buds sprouted anew.

I wish that I gave you flowers on Earth,

and not upon your tomb.

I wish that the flamboyant had bloomed sooner.

So, I could cut them for you and place them in cool water.

But none of these things happened before you died.

And if I knew you were going so soon,

I would have never said,

"Mother's Day will come again soon."

I would have made a bouquet that very day,

so now I wouldn't have to say,

"I wish that I gave you flowers on Earth

and not upon your tomb."

Suffering

I am determined not to suffer,
Not for man, woman, or child.

I am determined not to suffer, not even for a while.
I have watched too many loved ones sit silent as they
suffered in grief and in shame.

I am determined not to suffer,
I will not make my life harder for the comfort of another.

I am determined to live for me.
Because from what I have seen,
it is you who lay alone, cold and dead in your grave.

I am determined not to suffer,
not for man, woman, or child.
Because in the end,
those very people may not stay by your side.

I am determined to live my life for me,
because in the end.
The end is all you see.

What Happened After...

Their tears were criminal, a lie, a hoax intended on playing
cruel tricks on the very people who once cared for them.

My tears were genuine, and they cascaded along the
trenches of my face for what felt like an eternity.
There were only a few who stopped them,
there were only a few who cared.

Those who were silent remained silent
and used their silence as a weapon.
Those who spoke seemed as though they could only speak
of ignorance and folly.

Their convoluted conversations pierced deaf ears.
But whenever I could hear,
my responses were swift and sharp.

My fierce daggers stabbed deeper than expected.
Shocked, a few changed my name from *Sunshine* to "bitch."

I remained neutral on their verdict.
Their council did not dishearten me much,
for nothing they did or said after that point,
had meant anything to me.

This is what happened after you left.

Life

Life is ever changing,
it makes no sense to plan.

One day your head is above water,
the next, in sinking sand.

Life is ever changing,
and it waits for no man.

It can pluck you up and swallow you whole,
leaving only a corpse as a remembrance of your soul.

Life is ever changing,
it makes no sense to plan.

In a blink of an eye,
everything you had ever worked for,
can slip right out of your hand.

Nothing in life is for certain.
Not even life itself.

Life is ever changing.

Death

What cuts
deeper
than a
knife
and is sharper than a blade?

Death...

Death is a deafening numbing pain.

Take your last breath as the world around you
ceases to exist.

But life goes on and so does Death.

Your loved ones cry and mourn your loss,
while others try to count your rusted pennies at any cost.

But Death can't be the end, can it?

I know it cuts deeper than a knife.
But after Death, must come new Life.

A.D.

Aloes and advice
Precious moments in life
"He never leaves us nor forsakes us."
That's what you told me, right?

Bitterness and bereavement
Silhouettes on abandoned staircases
"I love you, but God loves you more."
Was one of your final statements.

Consideration and compassion
Quiet storms of any fashion
"Remember to give Him praise,
even on your lonely days."

Deliverance from despair,
Come only if you care.
Everlasting life is near,
it's time to go home now.

Part II.

For My People

"To be African American is to be African without any memory and American without any privilege."

– James Baldwin

Rooted

My roots have been tangled, teased and cut.

I have been uprooted from the land which has watered me
and taken to a land that does not understand what I am.

I am a beautiful gentle flower, a hibiscus.
But you handle me rough, a cactus.

You break and probe me for the little water I have left.

And without second thought I am laid to rest.

But my thorns, they are sharp and I regrow quickly.

But when I sprout and spread, you regard me a "nuisance,"
just remember, it was you who uprooted me,
and took away my true essence.

Carry On...

Most were dead upon arrival.
Others were bought as if they were animals.
Used and abused for centuries,
and yet, we carry on.

Carry on as if it didn't happen,
as if they did nothing wrong.
We speak about it seldom, if even at all.

For those who do speak,
are labeled "abrasive" and are dismissed
without second thought.

"Why are they still so angry?" some would query,
"Why are they so pissed off?

We are angry because of slavery,
rape, lynching, Apartheid,
Jim Crow, racism, police brutality, systematic racism,
and so much more.

We are angry because despite all of this,
we're still forced to carry on.

When We Were One

When we were one,
we spoke the same language
our tongues were in sync.

We were once brothers and sisters,
all from the same lineage.

Now we are just cousins,
twice removed.

We come from the same tree,
but bear very different fruit.

Your mother doesn't speak to mine,
they no longer see eye to eye.

"Our views are just too different,"
I heard said many times.

But to me there is no difference, a fruit is a fruit.

If we all come together, we could feed the multitude.

BlackNess

Black is bold
Black is gold

Black sits upon a throne,
it greets the world in different tones.

Black is unapologetic,
not just a color but pure genetics.

Black is deeper than the complexion of our skin,
and it's deeper than what the white man thinks is sin.

Blackness can be found in every inch of Africa,
in every river,
every stolen piece of gold and every stolen piece of land.

My blackness, our blackness can be found,
but it can never be sold, nor can it be borrowed.

My black is bold
My black is gold

Yes, I'm Mixed

I'm mixed with elixir and honey
Maubi and fungi
Tamarind and soursop

Yes, all that

I'm mixed with Queens and victory
All the lives you took from me
Ginseng and curry

Yes, all that

I'm mixed with history and rosary
Rosemary and aloe leaves
Sugar cane and slavery

Yes, all that

I'm mixed with blood and tears
Pomegranate and pears
Dandelion and fears

Yes, all that

I'm mixed with Christ and calypso
Ropes, chains, and disco
Africa and other islands tuh

Yes, all that

I'm mixed with the history
you gave to me, and the
history that I take back

Yes, all that

New Growth

I grew out my hair to find the new me.

The lye, dyes, perms, and texturizers
had begun to consume me.

Creamy crack had hair flowing to my back.
The pain from scrapes and burns had meant nothing to me.

I was hooked,
and like an addict, I kept going back for more.

Beauty is pain,
and I didn't want to lose the beauty I had once attained.

"But what if I go natural?"

Let my curls and coils
sprout and spread.

"Wouldn't I still be beautiful then?"

It took a while to see,
but If I didn't cut off dead ends,
I would have never grown to love the real me.

Protection

We install cameras,
lock and bar our doors.

We try to stay inside our homes,
it's where we feel protected the most.

We buy guns for security,
like loved ones, we keep them close.

But what if what we fear most, lies inside,
deep within our souls?

Our subconscious is our biggest enemy,
and it's so hard because in order to be a friend to you,
I must first become friends with me.

Part III.

For My Love

"Love takes off masks that we fear we cannot live without and know we cannot live within."

- James Baldwin

Two

My thighs are made for love,
my heart is made of strength.

Blood, love, and alcohol spilt on black cement.

Curved from years of pain,
my heart beats off tempo.

We swagger in and out of madness,
as our desires become deeper.

We are no longer one,
we are now individuals.

Completely separate but equal.

You go your way and I go mine,
yet we are still one.

One soul, two individuals.

Dream Catcher

In the abyss of your eyes,
I watch time fly as ponds turn to lakes.

The beauty of your journey inspires me,
I now follow dreams that many say don't exist.

But you believe, and that's all that matters to me.

You conjure up spells and slay dragons all just to follow those dreams.

I know you will never stop until every last star has been pulled out of heaven and those dreams come true.

And I will continue to believe in dreams,
because you believe in them, and I believe in you.

Crickets

Candlelight flickers.

Crickets call upon each other for companionship.

As we lay together, entangled.

We are not Adam and Eve, embarrassed.

The flesh we were given is the flesh we connect with.

Memories of past lives flash before your eyes,
as mine roll back.

They flutter like the butterflies do, on warm summer nights.

The ceiling fan rotates, cooling the flesh that is set aflame.

Your chest is like a drum, when the beating slows,
so do the crickets.

The candle is the only thing left lit,
as the flesh we connect with, cease to exist.

Rough Hands

Rough hands behind my back.
Blindfold around my eyes.
I bite down on my bottom lip,
trying to mask the swirl of pleasure and pain
that was brewing within me,
a hurricane.

There is nowhere for me to run.
I am pinned to the bed,
and it's not like I want to run, to be untied.
I had wanted every inch he had promised me.
every bite, I had begged for.

Rough hands tend to have the softest touch.
Nuzzle your head into the crook of my neck,
and tell me how much you like to…

You're in my sweet spot, between pleasure and pain.
I scream and I yell.
I curse your name to heaven and hell.

But you can't hear a thing.
You're in your groove, under my spell.
With your rough hands behind my back,
as mascara trails down my face.

Sunday Blues

Sunday blues give Monday a new meaning.
On Sunday we color the bed in blues and pinks.

On Monday we stagger out of bed,
still numb from what Sunday did to us,
from what we did to each other.

On Tuesday, once we've recovered,
we do it all over again.

But this is no routine.

The steam from between my thighs fog your glasses,
as you take your tongue for a swim.
You swim laps and then run them for what seems like hours.
We do this daily, nightly, and weekly.

But this is no routine.

Sunday blues give Monday a new meaning.

Intimacy

Intimacy
Talk to me
Tease me

When our souls collide, we become one.
It's like we were meant to be.

You caress my mind and body
You explore me until I explode

There is nothing more intimate than exploring a woman's soul...

Once upon a time

Once in every Black Queen's life,
She will fall deeply in love with a Black King,
and they will live happily ever after.

All of her dreams will come true
and she will center her heart around him.
It was God who created this union
and no one can tear them apart.

The storm that was once brewing within her, will cease.
And there will be a calm in her spirit.

Once in every Black Queen's life,
she won't have to question her purpose in another's.
He will reassure her with every touch, with every smile.

But life is no fairytale,
and nothing is perfect, nor is it certain.

But once the love is strong,
it can conquer any dragon that comes their way.

Once in every Black Queen's life,
she will fall deeply in love with a Black King,
and they will try to live happily ever after.

www.ingramcontent.com/pod-product-compliance
Lightning Source LLC
Chambersburg PA
CBHW071416290426
44108CB00014B/1851